VOICES & VENUES In VERSE!

Turn and Turns

By -
Kenneth J. Hesterberg

Copyright © 2023 by Kenneth J. Hesterberg

All rights reserved.

ISBN 978-1-62806-386-8

Library of Congress Control Number 2023916042

Published by Salt Water Media
29 Broad Street, Suite 104
Berlin, MD 21811
www.saltwatermedia.com

Cover photo, courtesy of:
P/C Nancy Lee Harvey; Cambridge Sail and Power Squadron

Primary Editor: Janet Jones

The Turning Time

The unbelievable word of Turn,
And, it's plural Turns__
How little we think about them,
But, "they" in many ways__ rule our lives!

Turn around! Turn in,
Turn out__ Turn down__
Turn right! Turn left!
Or you can even "turn-up.

Or is that turnip!
My father would say,
They go with mutton.
Never would, could or will I,
Agree with that.
But turnips mashed with potatoes,
Are, a pretty good dish.

Let's, turn too__
And understand, "Turn and Turns,"
Have very few limits imposed,
And play a role,
In the making of each and every
Day, of our existence
The wondrous minutes and hours,
We are to know.

"Believe it, or Not__"
Is a "Turn" to make!

Dedication

To those, who walk among us,
Who look not for medals and fame,
And, yet in their quiet way serve humanity__
Let them find solace in the words:
"The meek shall inherit the Earth."

For, if any so deserve,
Recognition from fellow humankind,
These are those,
Who should never have to stand in line.

And, to all of those,
Who, choose to help, and mentor me
Throughout my life,
Many known and unknown,
Un-thanked, but not unappreciated
I extend:
My gratitude and approbation,
And hopefully, God on high,
Will recognize,
The challenge of their effort.

ב

Turn or not to Turn

Why "Turns,"
As a "Title; why not?
It forecasts the principles and actions,
Applied to find, prosper and hold,
Your path to good living.

Very seldom is life and living
A straight line.
And a "<u>turn or turns,</u>" well done,
Help make the reality of living
A **Turn** well begun.
Find in the verses, bits of wisdom there for you!

ב

Table of Contents

Prologue	13
Turns	14
A, Turn of Truth	16
Concerns	17
Warning Signs	18
Reminders to Remember	19
A Turn Made	20
Turn Around	20
Turn About	21
Today's Prayer	21
Two Kinds of Love	22
Conscientious Choices	23
Yours by Right	24
Advice	25
The "Ides of Life"	26
Perfection Supplied	28
Answering Machine Humor	28
And Another	28
Ferret out the Fiends	29
A Point to Remember	30
Facts	31
Travel	32
Given Thought	34
The Value of Truth	35
A Fact to Deem	35
Random Observations	36
Machine Humor again	37
On the Waters	38
Adventure Awaits	40
The World of Water	41

A Sailing Turn	42
William James Ogle	43
Made and Making	44
The Process	45
Notes in a Journal	46
Rings and Things	47
My Gone Gal	48
Look Around	50
Listen "Pilgrim"	51
Timely Turns	52
Turning Times	53
Thoughts in Time	54
Truth Abounds	55
Turns in Retrospect	55
A Premise Grand	56
Turn Not, a Deaf Ear	57
Turn Back the Time	58
A Different Thought	59
Nature's Nurture	60
Word Play	61
Always to Defend	62
Judgment	63
March of Time	64
It's, how you see it	65
Verse, the Virus in me	66
Another Thought	67
Twists and Turns	68
Prayer Time	68
Life's Road	69
When, Two, Become One	70
Clear Thought	71
Growing Times	72

Taking, a "Turn"	74
Dogs of War	75
A, Thought	75
Boater's Blues	76
"Turn," Back Time	78
Talent in Turn	79
Green Wood Telegraph	80
Statements	82
One-Minute, Review	83
An Old Man's Ramblings	84
A, Turn of Truth	86
Heed	86
Do a Good Turn	87
Free Advice	87
A Question Asked	88
Words Overheard or Said	89
Write Now	90
Tick Tock	91
Time to Turn	92
Turn On	93
Science doesn't, Lie	94
"Understand"	95
Possible or Not	96
"So"	97
The Circle of Life	98
All Depends on Choice	99
Always, a Surprise	100
Seeing Memories	101
Time for a Turn-around	102
Rhetorical	103
A New Leaf, to Turn	104

Other Books by KJH in the series: VOICES & VENUES IN VERSE!

The World of Water: Fair winds and foul, beacons, lighthouses, on ocean, rivers and bays, or in the deep!

Yesterdays, Other Days and Holidays: Holiday's of humankind, Tributes, Recognitions & Remembrances!

Inspiration: Thoughts the additive, for the engine of humankind!

Inspiration Two & Too: Self-motivation through life!

Moments in Time and Scope: Memories, ideas, capacity for achievement, vastness for self!

Of People and Spaces: Space like most things in life, only a restriction of the human self!

Choices, Chances & Life: Choices- to make! Chances_ one takes! Life_ a gift of worth!

VISTAS: Visions of the beholder, seen, felt & sensed, memory markers!

Tapestry of Life Spun: Woven through ones life, how good when done, depends on the path chosen!

Earth Tones: Majestic in color & sound, there, where ere you go_ your gift!

Earth Rhythms: Earth's rhythms playing on this planet's scene, there to grab and hold!

Rebound: A skill to perfect, to better your life!

Baker's Dozen: When a Dozen, become 13, with short stories in Verse, to touch, your heart, soul and mind!

XIV: A tribute to days when numbers, were letters, and no zeros could be found!

The Gathering: Of, like groups human and non-human, together find a kindred ship!

Perambulation: If you think you are not in life's parade, how foolish you are!

Perception: A gift at birth, helping to make each day the best it can be!

Diversity: Life's colors, sounds, feelings and times!

Intuition: Perhaps a touch of magic, or ESP, or remnants found in one's DNA!

Mélange: This, that and the other", to capture your invested moments!

Turns: Actions that influence the direction of life!

The following, written and awaiting publication!

"A Moment in Time" Are gems to hold and serve for a lifetime.
"Bees, Trees and Butterflies" These are, true gifts from God.
"The Time Before" The springboard, for all of life's days to come.

Cover photos of all Books, in the series, (except Perambulation) are waters near the Chesapeake Bay_ My, muse since childhood.
The verses "Short Stories" meant to be read, throughout life!

Prologue

I awoke in the middle of the night,
Not unusual in my life
And, when I do,
I must arise and put in ink__
The thoughts that made awaking so.

On that particular night
The words "Turn and Turns,"
Drove me from my bed,
Soon, a full page was scrawled
In my chicken scratch!

And, as the weeks went by,
I added, many more verses related to:
The "Turn & Turns in Life."
More, than I ever thought cogent or possible.
Each verse, stirred an awareness,
Of the role, these two words play in all lives.

Think you, about the "Turns" in your life,
And, how those words, serve your every breath.

ↄ

Turns

In addition to the natural phenomena,
Like Earth's Tones and Rhythms,
That are, present__
In and around this planet__

There are the physical aspects__ of humankind,
Which, play unnumbered__
Roles, in the lives of humanity.

Take the **"turns"** one makes,
Many times, without thought,
That, has positive or negative influences__
Now, and in the future,
On each and every human.

My turn, his turn, her turn, your turn__
Many times, life doesn't seem fair,
Like for example,
Not every being__ gets a turn at being born.

Some never catch that first breath,
Others a breath or two,
And then no more!

And, still others,
Get too many turns__
It might seem, to you and me!

Life and living are,
Strange and wonderful gifts.
And "turns' come up,
And, sometimes disappear__
Before, recognized and utilized.
And there are, times,
You have to fight for your turn__

And other times,
When you are glad__
Your turn, just wasn't next!
Turns, an interesting concept,
A sort of "brotherhood example"
Of people with a conscience__
Who, understand that all,
Should__ get his or her__
Turn or turns, in life.

But, turn and turns,
Help make the world go round.
Think about the turns in your life__
How many have you taken?
What, role or roles, did your turns play?
Turns all have a measured impact,
In every moment of life!
Yes, you can have a turn
Make, a turn, give a turn,
Turn to, turn away, or turn into.
But, know always:
For a turn, or turns to take,
One must measure the when, where,
How and which turn to take__ or pass.

But here is a final thought__
"Everything gets its turn to die."
Funny isn't it some don't want that turn,
And there are others, wishing__
Their turn__ was then and now.
Turn, turns, and turning__
most likely more__
Than you ever gave thought.
Perhaps, if not__ now is the time;
To "turn" off the light,
And sleep, while it is your Turn.

↺

A, Turn of Truth

I have spoken of this before.
I do so for music is much on my mind:
No true musician, will I ever be__
But, to read musical notes,
A, true joy, would be.
Then, I could follow,
The parades of music played;

Unfortunately, I have little talent
For an, instrument to play,
Or, read the notes jotted down.
And, in this life,
I understand__
For me, it will always be, this way.

But some talent I possess__
And lyrics at times I write,
Stealing the notes from others
Oh, but in this life of mine
I am surrounded with talent
And take it no further, than
To bring my lyrics alive for me.

For at least the beat is mine,
And the music is held in my mind.
To recall, if, and, & when__
And, so grateful am I,
Others, share with me,
Their music and talent__
That, brighten the days. Of humanity.

What a world, in which to be__
Ah yes, what a world.

ㄅ

Concerns

I have come to the conclusion
That **Eden,** so often spoken of,
on this, planet Earth_ in reality.
Is not one place. but many
In areas throughout this Orb.

We, the present residents,
Have and are doing,
A poor job (to say the least),
In serving as "caretakers,"
On this planet, we call Earth.

And, if it had not been,
A heavenly appointed position_
Most would have been fired,
And sent packing_
To the Devil's den.

We desecrate Earthly beauty,
Pollute_ its waters, contaminate its air
Overheat its atmosphere,
Flush plastic down rivers,
And further denigrate without thought.

How foolish is humankind?
To think there is not a price to pay_
And those who will pay the most,
Are the unborn, innocent generations.
Of the tomorrows to come.

Tis, time to **"turn"** in the right direction_
And, do what is ours to be done.
To make every Eden on Earth whole again!

ב

Warning Signs

"Crazy Weather" worldwide;
Problems & challenges on every side,
Stupid those, who deny Global Warming___
With, their need, to make every last dime.
As they put the Earth,
And its people in a deadly divide!
Whether you believe in GOD___
As a "him or her" or not in GOD; at all___
Best put your faith, in something or someone,
For man didn't make this Earth___
That humankind is just pulling down,
And best understand, time now___ is running out.

So, hear & heed, some common sense
And, for proof of the truth,
Just look around___
As stories worldwide___ come forth,
With, death and destruction, taking place;
Know you and yours___ could be next.

From the beginning,
When leaving the swamp of birth,
Humankind (theoretically) knew or felt___
Through fear and awe, there was something,
Out there, greater than he and she!
Is it not time,
Once again, for all to bow down
And recognize, "something" is out there,
Call it God, or any name you choose___
But, work the plan, so devised,
And save this Earth for today___
And for, generations, yet to come.

כ

Reminders to Remember

When born__
We begin this journey on **borrowed time,**
And travel through the years and decades,
Allotted, for us to find.

Till then comes the day__
We can borrow no more;
And life for us__ is over and done.

However; what we did,
With the time allocated;
Has had a great deal, to do
With, what we've, become.
And, how we are, perceived, by others__
Plays a part, of our legacy when gone.

So, think not,
That you have lived life on your own
For that would be, a big mistake.
Tis a village, and hundreds of others,
That helped mold you__
Into the image, seen before life. is done.

So, know this,
You have a role, to play in this world.
And, you'd better understand__
There are mentors and untold others,
Not to be forgotten,
As your "turn" begins__ to mentor others.

Just thoughts to help you__
Chart a course__ to repay, what you were given.

ׅב

A Turn Made

I took a "turn" the other day,
And, found myself,
About five miles away__
Enjoyed the walk__

But, remember much of it not,
Day dreaming, I guess__
This, a concern, I must confess,
Makes me wonder,
What surprises will come next.

Life is sure a BLAST.

↺

Turn Around

If you take a "turn",
And find it's wrong,
Wait not__ but "Turn Around."

And, try another.
For a wrong turn, uncorrected__
Can lead to, a problem or more.

Thus, a choice to change,
Can be a boon__
To better your life for sure.
Or at least__
Time, to continue living__ some more!

↺

Turn About

"Do a *Good Turn* Daily"
The youngest of Boy Scouts,
Have for a century more,
Learned, from their very first day!
Tis a motto strongly supported,
In his and now her, Scout ways.

And, that is a lesson,
Each in their life, throughout
Hopefully__ a habit makes
Ingrained, included, indispensable__
Always.

Many times, unknown and unseen__
Too bad, most of the population,
That motto never_
Learned or practiced daily.
What a better world, could be,
If all a good turn daily, would do & see.

↺

Today's Prayer

Thank you, "Lord' for another day,
Hopefully some good I can do__
For others on my way.

And, maybe learn how better to be,
In serving you, and all__
Throughout my Earthly stay!

↺

Two Kinds of Love
(And, don't you forget it!)

The first is governed,
By chemistry and emotion__
And, can last for a day,
Or even generations.
Could be, of the same gender!
And, for others__
Looking, just for, cohabitation__
Or, a life-long commitment.

Now the second type of love,
Not necessary, a separate entity.
And, this one is founded__
On common sense,
And, deep admiration!

Of one or some,
Form of recognition,
With a bond
Of mutual, understanding.
And with no sex delineation.

These are types of "Love"
Of distinct amalgamations__
Can be separated or compounded,
Seen, in the human also animal kingdoms__
Many times, of lifetime duration.
And a friendship,
Where no distance, is considered.
Can, make breathing worth__
The trouble of daily living.
See, how simple the explanation,
Of what is, was, or can be__
A complicated conundrum.

Maybe, even__
In, a truthful application;
Of the two types of love
As, one, or both or together.

Ah Love,
What a complicated emotion.

↺

Conscientious Choices

Your choices in life__
The kind of road, you will travel__
That trip has already begun.
Think with wisdom, of your destination
So little time is wasted, on life's run.

Pick carefully, your direction, chosen,
Roads go many ways__
What seems the best, is not always;
For, life, in truth, tends either__ up or down.

Tis, in the after-life,
Final judgments are considered;
The trip up is the prize,
Bad choices, sends you down.

Let your conscience guide your journey,
When your "turn" comes around__
After once underway,
There are few transfers allowed__
Unless life, has played__ an unkind hand!

↺

Yours by Right

It happens in each generation,
In teens, we, feel smarter than parents__
By the time we are twenty,
We think__ we **"know it all."**

And the older generations__
Get frustrated, for they know,
The 20 something's__
Are, just beginning to know.

Many of that older group,
Just smile and" turn" away.
How foolish are those,
That listen not__ to what the elders say.

This is no different,
From generations that came before.
But, with the latest group or so,
There is a problem for sure.

Most of the younger generations,
Think, they are **"entitled,"**
To all the **"blood stained,"** good things__
That were earned before.

They won't agree, but it seems to me,
If all would sit down, and watch:
"A Tree Grows in Brooklyn," In "black & white"
How much they could learn, in one night.

Everything they take for granted,
Was earned, with the proverbial
Blood, sweat and tears__
Not by them__ but, those that came before.

And, just like "Freedom__"
Nothing is free, but must be__
Re-earned__ every day.
And that, which each new generation__
Gets to use, requires an honest, thank you__
To, most, who now inhabit. a grave.

Part of being: is, Common Courtesy,
Common Sense, respect for the elders,
Who have paid__ their dues__
By providing, many of the **"stepping stones,"**
Each, new generation. gets to use
Before their own, are ready to be laid!

And even though, not a mirror image,
Those here now, were the new not long ago.
Who helped make life, a bit easier,
For the next, generation, to come__
As other ancestors did, before they came.

No, nothing is free,
Except the breath God gives,
To start all on their way,
And, even that, is a debt to be repaid.

It is "the turn," for the "new", to do the same, with "grace__"
And to repay, a debt that is due!

ב

Advice: In the time it takes__
To look each way, is time well spent__
For an accident denied, is a, problem saved!

ב

The "Ides of Life"

Remember, from school days,
Shakespeare's "Julius Caesar"
And, the line: Et tu Brute"
As he lay dying,
It was, the Ides of March.

Funny about the word: **"ides"**
As used in the old
Roman Calendar__
It's mostly lost, in usage today__
It's meaning: is: the, "middle."

And in that Roman calendar__
(Unlike our calendar today
Changed in the 1750s)
The 15th was the Ides of:
March, May, July and October,
But, was the 13th of the other months
As, recalled, in the annals of time!

Never thought of it much,
And yet it has,
Played a role, in this life of mine.

My birth on the ides of September,
On the Roman calendar.
Our wedding on the "ides" of October,
My military discharge on the "Ides" of February
And, a paycheck, monthly on the ides.
And time and again appears, in my life!

Have you ever thought,
How the "ides" affects your life?
Most would never know, nor care.

About, the "Ides" of their longevity__
For it truly cannot be computed,
Till after the day of demise.

But, suppose we could,
And, it did matter,
As a reference point
And, chance to better our lives.

Perhaps now, a time, to analyze
And, actions take
With a goal of "betterment" at stake.

To do better, this time,
Knowing what we know,
And each time__ "Ides" comes into sight!

It's a thought,
A possibility, a potential,
Perhaps, a chance,
To baffle, and confuse,
Those, who see "Ides" for naught,
And, we__ a plus to our legacy, get.

"Ides" in our calendar today,
Eleven out of twelve,
The 15th, almost a perfect display!

Except for February,
When three out of four years,
Fourteen would be, the Ides at play!

Perhaps if recognized, "Ides" is truly a special day__
"Turn To" and see if "ides" can do for you.

↺

Perfection Supplied

Good News, there is a way,
That you can be mistake-less,
Think about it__
Never making a mistake again!
Why, you can brag,
How smart you are__
And no one, can that deny.
All you have to do is "Die."
↩

Answering Machine Humor

If you should dial my land line,
And, no pick up, you get__
If you wait for a couple moments__
A, message do leave for me to get.
And, I surely will call you in time__
Unless you are asking for money__
Then before you hear my voice,
You will be, deaf, dumb and blind!
↩

And Another

I spent my last dollar, today at the store,
I thought peanut butter and jelly,
Would be a treat__ like years before.
But, didn't have enough money__
To buy both at the same time,
So, make a guess,
Which on tonight's menu will be mine?
<u>Wrong: I'm coming to your house; to dine.</u>
↩

Ferret out the Fiends

I took some time, to ponder a while__
And, thoughts accumulated, in my mind.

It was then, I realized__
Humans, on occasion (?), are exceedingly gullible.
For many times, they take for granted__
What is read and heard,
Instead of thinking through__
The "disinformation", so many like to spew.

Accepting facts as they are__
Is, many times, easier than expending, thought.
Not all are guilty of this misdemeanor
But, look around you, to take note,
Of what is there__ that is worth naught.

So, put a question mark__
When, facts they come to you as true,
Because one never knows,
When someone is trying, a "con" or scam on you.

The world is full of those,
Whose, conscience is flawed__
And see you as their mark for that day.
Investigate, illuminate, examine with care__
Each word, with guile, the tune they play.

And when you ferret out,
The truth, or the lies they say__
If lies__ tell all the game, they tried to play__
Perhaps, put them where they have no say.
Just a thought,
For, a better world, you could assay.

ב

A Point to Remember

Here is a thought or three,
For you to ponder, if you would.

"Memories: the repository of life's happenings."
Very profound indeed, I am sure, not original,
The word history, is a could be.

But perhaps, easier to remember,
Than others, you have seen or heard.
Good, bad or in between, From youth, till life is done__
They, memories remembered, and stored__
To wait__ "retrieval."

But the hardest thing about memories__
Is keeping__ them absolutely TRUE.
Never adding, "polish" to shine on you!

So, let no lies taint the purity
Of moments captured
Throughout your life and living time.
For like a snowflake,
No two will be exactly the same.

Never duplicated, or replicated,
But new__ each to try__
Time & Nature makes, for change to find.
Memories, in true detail,
Are: gold and jewels, and dollars, in a bank__
To withdraw, as you the reason find.

To review, and lock away, again__
Until, wanted to be recalled.

Capturing them__ is God's gift to you;
Waste not the gift of time__
But, make as many memories,
As sanity and you, are willing to find.

And, keep a log, with adequate details,
To aid you in recall__
As the fog of years, counts out the time!

Thoughts, perhaps for you, to "<u>turn too</u>"
To utilize now, or at a future time!

ס

Facts

What I know, I truly know,
That I (like you), live on borrowed time__
When that time, gets canceled,
Is a date, "we" may one day know.
For, tis, just a part of life and living.

But that, worries me not.
However; I do sure hope,
It's not too soon__
For I still have much, I would like to do.

And, have Season Tickets
For when the Baltimore Colts come home.

Just a reminder, make every day__
The best day you can.
But, unfortunately
It can never be, exactly the same again!

ס

Travel

In places near and far,
Where ere you "turn" On this Eastern Shore,
"Delmarva" a title claims
And three states, lands do name!
Of Delaware, Maryland and Virginia
Are spots for us, historical to view.

Not like in Europe,
Many hundreds or millennia old
But places, with markers of
birth and buildings__
A piece of a Nation of principles;
Not yet fully clarified__
But changing to meet the tides of time.

We, if wise can find,
Many pieces, and sites,
From four or five centuries behind__
Many rebuilt by those,
Who, understood
Ones' total history must be known.

Facts, both the good and bad,
And, the in between,
But, for the stability of "tomorrow,"
The past must be recognized and claimed.
While, these verses speak to The Eastern shore,
Of the Chesapeake Bay,
History was written throughout,
This land we now call the USA.

So, to make an even better tomorrow__
Put on some comfy clothes,
And, a good pair of walking shoes.

Then go see your history__
Learning from books is fine,
But seeing, feeling and being,
Will touch your soul and mind.

All was not good,
Here and everywhere,
Neither then, nor today__
But ferreting out true history,
Is, a start to assure__
A better tomorrow, be arrayed.

Conscience and full truth, should be,
The writer of forward history,
That is ours, this day to decide.

Chaos, bigotry, greed,
And others to name__
Are, a pox on a better world to find.
The answer perhaps Common Sense
Which at this time,
Seems to be in short supply!

And Common Courtesy,
Its death we must defy.

Time for all "to take a Turn,"
And, do what must be done__
For, future generations yet to come,
In a land, still young__
But where much history, does abide.

So be it__ say the wise!

ב

Given Thought

Just think of this__
All that humankind would have to do
Is, "*turn*" to the clues,
Already in plain view.

Provided by those, whose graves,
With markers exposed__
Who, have died, for me, and you!

Those many battles fought__
With so much talent lost
And, sadness, never truly explained.

They, played the game__
And say, listen, and follow me, not
But, do what your conscience,
Tells, you in truth!
While others,
Just seek the next battle to be got!

Brotherhood, no matter how hard
A mouthful to chew,
Is, the only answer__
For, a world of fairness to view.

Think this not__
That you, and yours,
Be no better, and learned no more,
Than those, who came back, from wars before.

Tis up to "we" to find a way, to make__
A better world, for us, and those coming, one day.

ל

The Value of Truth

If we stand not for "Truth."
Nor stand not to be counted__
We are but a crashing cymbal,
Or a clanging bell.

And, then comes a day__
The piper must be paid.
And, all will know, and debit you,
With things that should have__
In truth been__ told, but never done.

Yes, the lies do stay,
Marked, in a column made.
For all to see, and wonder why.

Listen, and obey__
Your conscience will know__
And, most likely,
Save you pain on life's road too know!
For, truth is the direction, to "turn."

ڂ

A Fact to Deem

Life and living,
Is, an arena, of constant challenge.
Where all must be prepared__
For the aggressor__ to face.
So, keep your mind, on the battle, to be won!

ڂ

Random Observations

I cannot tell you this,
Nor tell you that,
But what I can tell you,
The world is not flat__
And, that is that.

I can tell you day is light,
And, night is night,
And the stars are up,
And a hole that is dug goes down,
And, wind can blow 360° around.

And some people are good,
And others are bad,
And some days I'm happy,
And others I am sad__
And, most people find, this the same.

And, most smart folks, will__
With what I have stated, Without question,
With me__ agree.
That makes them smart__ you see.

Now a "Brain Surgeon", I will never be.
Nor other things, that come to mind,
But still GOD, has patience with me__
And, gives me leave,
For a life to find.

Funny, how the earth goes around,
And "Mother Nature" dictates so much to all.
What a "grand "turn" life provides__
With birth, and living,
Plus, great, opportunities to find.

Are your observations__ like mine?
Or is this just a conundrum
Where an agreement__ is hard to find?
Is it, like, an enigma, to puzzle your mind__
Till an answer, comes down the line.?

If there is enough time,
Will every answer come to your mind?
Or are you a "human" just trying to get by?

And, thoughts like these, boggle you mind?
Worry not, just words to keep you alive.

ὐ

Machine Humor again

I'm too busy,
Won't answer the phone,
So, get off the line,
And leave me alone!

And, if you won't go away,
A, message, leave__
Unless money is your game__
Then, my, laughter is the answer you'll receive.

But maybe I will return your call,
How lucky you will be,
To hear from me at all.
By the way, this is a "Robo" call.

Beep!

ὐ

On the Waters
(For, boaters, one and all.)

More than some__
I dream of the romance of the sea.
To be on boats, is a place to be__
For those who immerse themselves,
In the lore, reality and love__
Of all waters, is an advocation to gain.

But with these thoughts,
And, hopes for waters to ply__
Comes the responsibility,
Of vast knowledge to obtain.
To learn the why and ways__
Of boats and seas, no lubber to be.

And, be not an onus__
To self and others,

As a, danger like__
A derelict afloat and free;
In crowded lanes and harbors,
A magnet, of death to see.

One, who steps upon a deck,
Needs more than basic knowledge,
And experience__ so not a danger__
To self and others, will collect.

And the learning thereof,
Is, a challenge__ but a fun-filled one__
To gain experience and know-how,
And to stretch abilities,
Useful for all times, on water.
Is, the **"Right Turn"** a course to come!

To slip a line, without knowing__
The way of a sea person.
To make yourself think.
You know enough,
And you know not__
Is a crime against humankind.

Is to put every boater on the water,
In, harm's way, and even if not__
You are rolling the dice,
With snake eyes, almost a 100% to find.

When many, courses of study,
So, easily available__
To Captain, crew, and new__

From the U.S. Power Squadrons,
The U.S. Coast Guard Auxiliary, and others__
There is no reason, not to be safe__
On waters far and wide.

True__ for any boater to be, on board
You, a fountain of knowledge__
Should be__ for you are:
Responsible for those,
Whose feet your deck, do trod.

And the water is to be respected
And realization must be__
That if in a motor vehicle,
And, an accident occurs__
There is a chance to walk away.

But from a boat, walking on water__
The last time heard, was the Fisher of Men."
More than 2,000 years ago, that ability applied.

ℶ

Adventure Awaits

The joy, wonder, and fun,
Of spending time on most__
Any floating marine "things,"
Is a memory to keep__
Treasure, and expand.

On the waters of the world,
The term "Rules of the Road"
Are, bundled to keep, a semblance,
Of commonsense practices,
In mind all the time.

On land there are "Rules of the Road,"
But differ on water, because of its fluid nature
No poured, asphalt lanes,
But buoys, and light houses, and nuances,

Charts and electronics, compasses,
A plenty, to help one keep a course__
From, port to port, or around the world.

Boating on the water is a different world,
And challenges all, in untold ways,
The ebb & flood, of tides,
Currents, winds, is__ life on the waters.

The fetch, of waters from distances away,
The beauty of sunrise and sunsets,
And challenge of nights under star filled skies.

The fishing, crabbing, exploring,
Of streams, rivers, bays, ports,
And rendezvous with fellow boaters,
Are, adventures, to proclaim.

ᴐ

The World of Water

Is three quarters of this Orb's surface.
Believe it or not, there are people,
Who never or seldom venture, upon it.
Those of us who do__ can only pity them.
And perhaps the non-boaters, Feel the same pity
For those whom the water beckons.

Each degree of the compass,
Sends one off, to a different course to chase__
To a port of call. or no port at all.
To a shallow river or Bay,
Or in the miles of deep depth of an ocean,
Where one has, storms to tend,
Or windless, expanses to endure.
The waters of the world, one and all,
Paint, a life, worth the time to live.

Yes, the water from rills, to streams__
And, bays or oceans found,
Go from inches, to thousands of feet down.
And there are more in this animal kingdom,
In these, wetted reaches, than all the solid ground.
And once a wheel, or tiller is in your hand,
And you build a book of knowledge,
To understand boats, waters, and life,
On the wet, it gets, in your soul,
Hold on to it as long as you can.
Because a day will come,
As it does, with all,
When memories,
There TURN
To call.

ꙋ

A Sailing Turn

I sail today in memories and dreams
With, salty tears now shed.
Oh, to be back, on rivers,
Bays, and oceans again,
Where freedoms' feeling thrives__
But, know now those days,
Are, in the past,
And, no longer for me, do survive!

But, if I could, I would
For I miss the aroma,
That comes with the sea.
I miss the waves, and blowing gales,
That challenged me.
I miss the blue over head
Sharing painted sunsets,
Reflected in the waters found.

But there is a spot in acres green,
Where my wife,
And, oldest son, await for me__
To rest eternally!
Tis a pleasant place, shared
With other generations gone.
But, with no bay, or salty sea,
Just a stream over rocks does sing.

But, never thought,
When my time did come,
Ashes for me to make__
For that eternal rest.
For that was not the way,
Of my, generations passed__
But wonder if now,
It a thought for me, be best.

If, I could share, my love for both,
Some in woodland solitude,
And, some in the tides to ride__
How better could that be?
But, if only one could make__
No question, my "bride" I take,
And, let my love of sea and sail,
Die with me!

**How are you faring,
As you, your final decision you try to make?
Leave it not to another, that choice to take__
Tis your "turn" this course to steer!**

 כ

William James Ogle
(1877 – 1945)

I shared time with him,
For almost 11 years,
Before his passing.
His death preceded,
By months, the end of WWII__
And I miss my Pap, even today.

Years after his passing,
On a visit to his grave,
A hole had opened large__
Enough for me to see his casket
(No crypts in those days).
I reported it, and the hole was filled.

But I often wondered__
If he came back, just me to see.

כ

Made and Making

How much of life is missed,
When, truth in history is dismissed?
For if one knows not__
The truth, the whole truth,
Of the times and its doings,
One becomes a fool, And, destined,
To prove that assertion,
Beyond any shadow of doubt.

For it is known,
If humankind, learns not from history
All are doomed to repeat it again,
And, again, and again.
And this a detriment__
In every breath humanity takes.
These be not just words,
But signs on a path to mediocrity.

If you learn nothing else "Humankind,"
And, take no other action in life,
Learn and change,
The bad habits, earned over millennia,
And its pension to defy History,
If not__ the demise on the horizon,
Promised and foreseen,
Is nearer at hand than you dream.

The good, here on earth,
Has only been scratched,
The abilities of "man"
Are, unfathomable.

But, "a path" to complete loss__
Is built longer each day.

See what history shows,
Hear what History speaks,
And, do what you know__
Has to be done.
For, history, is the "Seer"__
Of life, not yet done!

っ

The Process

Through millennia's, history__
The future most times is predicted,
And, will surely come!

For no matter how hard,
The past, when present__
Captures the facts witnessed__
And, these, recorded and written.
Future generations__ eagerly forget__
So, once again, Satan, his song is sung.

With stupidity__ the words, man hums__
As he beats the drums, and war comes.
How sad this must be__
For the Deity in heaven above.

To note "his or her" children's__
Gross ignorance,
That seems, cannot be overcome.
What, wasn't learned through history,
Is doomed to be repeated, adnauseam__
Again, and again and again!

So, says, the sages in their time!

っ

Notes in a Journal

Well, it was Sunday again__
Cool to cold, but the sun shining;
Up early a tub of laundry in,
Dishes done—computer on__
Lots of rough verse typed.
It's funny how some days,
Never enough time to transcribe__
And then, not a line of verse will arrive.

Best of two worlds these days
Enough dollars from retirement__
To get by; and books to write__
And profits to those, who do "good for many."
I don't know about you,
But, when I am helping others,
I feel like my time here, is well applied.

I turn on the Sunday CBS News Show,
Always outstanding,
With life here and around the world.
It is something like a good sermon,
To make you think and, appreciate.

And at 10:30 I am off to PK,
For breakfast, and a closer look,
At my fellow humans__
And hear, see, and learn,
How I, myself can be a better__
Person, citizen, and Christian,
As I strive, to live, "The Golden Rule__"

Hope things for you, always "turn out" well.

↺

Rings and Things

I looked at my left hand this AM,
And, it was void of my wedding ring__
Not because, I wanted it to be,
But Arthritis, has become__
My mortal enemy.

But, for me fortunately,
There are days
When it can again be worn__
And, I feel good on those, mornings.

Almost 58 years together we were__
Until death took her away.
Come the "Ides" of October,
Tis another anniversary,
Of when my bride and I wed.
In 2022, it would have been, 67 years
How those many years, have sped away.

However, on those days,
When that Gold Ring I can don__
So many, great memories arrive;
Blessed I am, for the great run,
We did have and shared.
And, when my time does come__
Next to her, I hope, to lie,
Throughout the bye and bye.

"Yes, rings and things, and times recalled,
Make the days I live, worth living,
For, I was lucky, in the draw,
And, I pray__ she felt lucky too."

↺

My Gone Gal

(Thinking, of what could have been__
Had my Bride not passed.
Written on what would have been__
our sixtieth anniversary: Oct 15, 2015.)

As the following words came to me,
I couldn't help but think,
Of those many friends,
Who now, have lost a loved one too.

And who, perhaps,
Feel somewhat like I do,
As, life does go on,

And, I do look forward,
As the sun, gives me a start
For, each__ new day.

And I know my Bride
Urges me to live, for the two of us.
But, hear the truth I say__
How much, my heart is missing her.

No, you were__ never to go,
It was me__ if that had to be,
But God took you__ instead.

Yes, the days__ they come, and go,
Heaven, knows I'm missing you so__
And, nothing seems to feel just right.

Your last note I found__ just yesterday,
I cried, at the words, you did say,
"My darling, our vows no longer apply__
Live fully, before you die."

But, my love,
I don't want to take my Wedding Band__
From my finger, to put it away.

I love you more each and every day
And, tomorrow, I will again celebrate,
The anniversary, of our Wedding day.

This world, is as cold as it can be,
Life more, I am not sure I wanted to see,
Without you, empty all living seems to be.

I thank God for my dreams at night
For in them, I can hold you tight,
For that little while, the world seems right.
I know, I should, and am grateful for
Those years, we shared:
It was a gift__ but still I yearn for more.

Be patient with me__ love of mine
As, I try to find, a world that's new;
A world, no longer of me, and you.

I do remember, what you said to me,
And, do what I can__
To make life better, for all I see.

In honesty, I am doing things,
I never thought before to do__
One__ I am I writing, books in verse!

Unfortunately, none "she" will ever see__
But they make time, worthwhile;
And, help others, in ways, that pleasure me.

ↄ

Look Around

Spin a "Turn" style__ for a time,
Lie down and turn over,
Then turn upside down__
Eat a "turnover__!"
Let the crumbs fall, for ants to find.

Turn, the corner (in your mind).
Keep turning until__
There, are no more turns,
You want to find.

Then just think,
One day for me and you__
Sod will be "turned."
That for the last home to be found.

Then with kith and kin,
Turn up, for a reunion to have__
And maybe there will be
Some more turns, to grab,
Throughout time__
That, we won't know, until we do.

Who, knows
When it is, your turn in line__
Maybe not for a long, long time,
Then, that might be, a Good Turn
You will have to decide.
Turn and turns__ wow, how many in a lifetime,
Needing attention and a decision.
Maybe too few, who knows?

↺

Listen "Pilgrim"

I cannot understand__
Why, man, nee humankind,
Hears, sees and notes, not__
That, " Mother Nature" is always in command.

Weather, if it is calm or full-blown,
She; Mother Nature, can make a call,
To the frustration of; humankind__
Who, always wants to be, in command.

Few even try to understand,
And, those that do__
Face belittling pressure,
In forms__ old and new!
And in semi-silence,
The problems brew and brew.

Then admitting it or not, we know,
Soon, the end of humankind,
Will come__ if nothing, is done__
For Global warming, and Climate Change__
Are factors leading to our demise.

So, "Turn To" Speak Out, and Reach out__
And, play a role, in saving,
Planet Earth__ this "EDEN" among the stars.
That can still, be a gift, for generations to come.

Only fools would lose,
Such a gift, granted__ for the cost of__
Each, serving, as a "Caretaker,"
Of this "Eden," in the sky!

ꕀ

Timely Turns

Most claim, they have no time,
And, that is something,
One must discuss with God. or another__

For between birth and demise,
Hopefully, adequate time is supplied,
For each human's, personal ride__
Or call it LIFE, if you must.

And while you cannot make time,
You can take time,
To do what must be done.
To make life, worth living.

Taking time, is an investment,
If for what, it is taken,
And pays dividends,
Because, it was wisely chosen.

But to, arbitrarily__ waste time
Is a sin, requiring, payment in kind.
For time is a gift from GOD,
That, one day, the "piper" will exact his due__

Much better, not to waste in the first place.
Mortal you be,
Till no more mortality, you see.

So, sit quietly, for a moment,
And, think how better,
Your given time can be applied.
Better for you, on Life's timely ride!

ᓂ

Turning Times

Seconds, minutes and hours,
Make days,
Days, become weeks and months,
Then, "turn" into years,

And, years have, twelve "Ides."
The old time, middle of the month.
That was used, for many reasons found.

Ides; were more important, back when__
The calendar, differed from today
Ides, written, and prized, for the clarity found.
In ancient history,

But at times, Ides still used today.

Think you__
If all knew the Ides of one's life,
Would take the time to,
Review the first half of being__
And truly, plan for a better 2nd half.

What accomplishments
Would, and could be seen,
Throughout the rest of life's game!

My mother born, on the "ides" of the 9th month,
And me, wed on the Ides of the tenth!

Worth the time, you to examine__
How that mid-day of the month;
The "ides" touch your life?

ߘ

Thoughts in Time

If, it was possible,
That "all" could,
And, would live and prosper__
In Brotherhood,
What would "ALL" be willing to do?

Like, live, a better life,
Throughout, their lives__
For, others who are yet, to come?

The promise has been there,
In all millennia__
The world has known,
And, yet humankind, walked away,
With misunderstanding,
And stupidity on their faces, shown.

Maybe not stupidity__
But, with avarice and bias,
And fear of the unknown.

Will GOD or a deity undeclared,
Finally determine,
The human experiment failed?
Then, cleanse this laboratory
called Earth__ and make it void?

Or can the human race,
Possibly be redeemed
Or is that a fate__ yet to be gleaned?

Perhaps, "brotherhood' truly could be__
And a whole new kind of world, be seen.

Truth Abounds

Another day and another dollar,
Only true, if a job you have;
For the many,
It's food stamps, food banks.
Not enough food, nor money__
The fight to live, a challenge always!

How can this be__
In a country where bounty is found?
Is it not time, instead of,
Sending money abroad__
We first, take care of "our own?
Or is it both__ we have to do?

ᗡ

Turns in Retrospect

Turns, like "Choices, Tones, & Rhythms,"
And the like, have a measured part,
In, each moment of life.
So, understand, you can have a Turn,
Make, a turn, give another a turn,
Turn to, Turn away and Turn into.

But, know always__
For any turn or turns to participate,
One must consider,
When, where, how and which__
Type of TURN, to, or not to take.
Ah, decisions, a conundrum,
A puzzle, a choice, as life dictates.

ᗡ

A Premise Grand

What, a gift humankind has__
On this fantastic rock called Earth.
We are allowed__ to "rent" space.
For a time, called Life.
And, if want or need more__
Able to "sometimes to squeeze out a bit more__
But are expected to be "<u>Caretakers,</u>"
Of this orb, throughout, our living days.

And each of us desire,
Whether, deserving or not,
To hold on to a piece, of the orb.
And, nurture our bit of "dust."
This, be our final measure,
Of our claimed right to exist.

The wise humans, among us,
Note there is little difference,
Among us, except "tint of skin."
For now, we have found__
Internals__ are interchangeable.

Too bad, most cannot see__
We of humankind;
Are, from the same "**<u>Tree of Life.</u>**"
And being, together__ may be our salvation__
For alone__ hasn't proven, our case.

And, were placed, in diverse locations__
To test the benefits, of each, though different.
Then at times we mingled;
Showing a need,
To better, understand, one another.

Yet at times, other positives found__
If we, look, beyond the outer skin,
Most of much of each, is the same.
Tis, acceptance, of and by individuals__
One on One, varied colors all__
Is the need for brotherhood!

Perhaps in a world of tomorrow,
Skin will just be that, as if the same__
No matter the tone it claims.
And, better will be life for all.
A way to go, but a "turn on" the right road?

Let us all, "turn" in the right direction
For, better world to seek__
And, If all could be good stewards,
To one another__ who knows,
What, in the world and life, could find.

ל

Turn Not, a Deaf Ear

Right turn, wrong turn
Conundrums throughout life,
Are, enigmas to solve!

Hopefully "you are"
Better than 500 hitters__
Or more pain, gained for you to resolve.

However, "turns" of all types__
Are daily in sight,
These, the dues to be paid__ for living, and life?

ל

Turn Back the Time

I pass the farms, the road does show,
Many, so many fewer now__
Than days, once, in youth were known.
Seems the kids, just want to grow and go.

I feel such a loss,
Perhaps, aging makes that so.
But worry the kids of today__
Will never know__ farmlands once did lend__
Pastoral beauty, so fine to know.

But in me sadness, like a pain abides,
When days before, were in time alive,
Oh, why does the world,
Feel the need of, changing so?

Me, I speak of farms,
But it's the whole damn world,
That I feel has erased the good, once known__
And common sense tells me,
My ancestors, rued the world,
Near the same way, as I do, this day,
But we as an average, live longer now,
And change is much faster__
And to me needlessly, abounds__
Why, can't life just slow down?

Maybe the younger, "ones" of today are right,
The old, live too damn long__ out of spite.
What are your thoughts__ thumbs up, or down.
I'd like an answer__
Could you kindly, put your cell phone down?

ꙅ

A Different Thought

A Poet is a poet,
Unless he or she is a Verse-ist!

Now the differences,
In Verse and true Poetry,
Are quite a few
And, here is just one thought to view.

Writers of verse, write always,
With rhyme and reason,
And in rhythm like a lyric of a song.

While a poet,
Sometimes, uses "Free Verse"
That many times rhymes__
With nothing one can find.

Then to this mother's child,
This is prose,
That anyone can write__
If given and taken enough time.

Both good__ take some thought,
And, quiet time__
But, speak differently.

Which, to like__ is up to you!
Me, a verse-ist, I am__
And will always, want to be.

But this is my choice, wouldn't you agree?

ᔐ

Nature's Nurture

Say Neighbor, look at Nature with care,
And realize, how much you could learn,
About life on this planet Earth__
If Mother Nature, you would study, and not spurn.

For, the things in nature
Were here long before humans came__
Long, long before__

And, existed__ till many disappeared,
And, new species entered the scene__
And, found ways to survive.

But also realize in Nature,
There is beauty and loss,
And sadness and joy.

But for non-man
Nature is truly,
The survival of the fittest when found.

The small are brought forth,
And for a time prosper,
And then are eaten by the larger,
That, in turn are eaten by the even larger.

But species sometimes survive
Not eating__ one another!

Humankind,
Are, one of the very few
With a conscience__
To give life a different view,
And even some of these,
I question if that is true!

The thought is,
By watching Nature wisely,
We of humankind,
Can be an even better species,
Than we are in this day and time.

And today, **"wiser"** is the key word,
If only to stop,
Global Warming, and Climate Change.
Before **"extinction"**
Is the only word to apply.

Tis, time too TURN
All attention, to saving this planet.
For today__ and future generations;
Who hopefully will arrive, and survive.
And, its each "you" to make this become true.

ꖺ

Word Play

Small can be large,
When something smaller,
Than small, arrives on the scene.
The same can be said in reverse,
About large, to be called small,

When larger than large becomes,
The largest, to appear__
A play on words,
But when facts become clear__
The English language is grand.

ꖺ

Always to Defend

Freedom is not free,
It's a responsibility of you and me__
To re-win it each and every day,
For not a day passes by,
When someone won't try__
To take our freedoms away.

For in this great land,
Our ancestor, took fate in hand,
And faced up to,
The tyrants of the time.

And openly declared__
"With our rights, you not interfere,"
And, the first shot was soon fired.

And battles were hard,
And many, in death disappeared.
Then, from diverse European lands,
Others came and gave us a hand__
To win, our first true freedom found.
Well, almost all.

But allow me to tell you my friend,
The battles will never end,
For freedom as said,
Is never free__
And when you think it is,
Your freedom will soon__ not be!

All anyone has to do,
Is to count the grave markers,
The world through,
And the proof of what is stated,
Would, could, and should enlighten you.

"For, to live free, some will always die."
This has been the truth throughout time.
Sometime, maybe one day,
A "Turn Around," *and a new truth, will be* **found.**

ↄ

Judgment

Perhaps you think a Turn or Turns,
Are not, important premises in life.
Then you would be wrong.

So wrong:
Just ponder, turn key, turn out, turnover,
Or a turnover (one with icing).
Drive, the turnpike, go through the turnstile,
See what is on the "turn table.

What's coming at every turn?
Go by turns, in turn, turn back,
Turnabout (fair play and all),
The SOB is a Turn Coat,
Women always use__ a turn down.

Yes "Turn," a mighty four- letter word
(Or "Turns" if used).
And in combination with other words__
Is, a demand for action__
Throughout a lifetime!

"Turn and turns," helps assure, living well__
Are paramount;"
Until, that last breath is "turned" down!

ↄ

March of Time

Again, it is Sunday morning,
And, I am where I am,
On most Sundays,
And other days, to be named.

I am up early every day,
And, have been for years,
But more so,
Since my "bride' passed away.

For since that dark day,
I write verse,
Some, in each twenty-four__
Mostly, in the early morning hours.

For that is my time__
When the words will not hide,
And I can, short stories,
For books, ink down.

Now this was not my goal,
As years did unfold__
But happened after family & friends__
Said, your Christmas stories,
Should be in books, to be found!

I then thought, **"one and done."**
And, then something else,
A challenge would be.
To make use of the time__ after "she."

That was then, and this is now__
And more than twenty books'
I have penned.

And a friend suggested,
I sign and sell to help,
Support, worthwhile Organizations.
And, that I relish now, to be done.

Now, this is background,
My friend, to let you know__
Something like this, you can "turn-to,"
With whatever, projects please you.

Challenges make life, truly worthwhile__
And, helping others, (frustrating-at- times)
But more than not__ gives one a smile.

And, smiles,
Make every day better.

ב

It's, how you see it

Nothing lasts forever,
But, forever is an unmeasured time__
And, forever to me, not the same that you find.

But a friendship that weathers time,
Does stop when one or the other,
A breath can no longer find.

But it was forever to the one
Now lost to time__
Forever, a *"turn"* to keep in mind!

ב

Verse, the Virus in me

Some call me a poet,
That, I think not, am I,
A writer of verse more likely.

Who, with rhyme and rhythm__
And no free verse,
Put stories long and short,
Inked on paper, then in books,
A legacy of mine to find.

Now, not attempting,
To, start a war of words,
I try to set the precept straight__
And, I have no mind set__ against poets.

For without much remuneration,
Poets, struggle on__
And, in most cases,
So, few, of their books are adored.

Brave souls, Poets must be,
To do what they love,
For all of their hard work,
Little money, they seldom see.

I cannot speak for poets,
But many times, as writer of verse,
Awakened in the middle of the night,
I must rise, and write,
For if waiting for the sun to rise,
No words, will I find.

My work, touches yesterdays
Today, and days not yet known!

A devil's advocate at times I play
And verse then__
For the other side, do write__
An open mind__ is my right.

Many tell me, my words__
Inspire, fire, anger and insight__
And this is high praise,
For what I receive__ in signing and sales
I pass, any profits__
To, not-for-profits, to their delight!

It is my hope to break even,
So, more books I can buy__
To help organizations in whom I believe.
The publication cost, I cover, as a legacy.
My remuneration is the reader's enjoyment__
And also, that I get__ as a writer of verse!

It is true,
That, since the death of my wife,
I have been pleasured, this to do.
How many books I will write__
I know not__ for age is fast coming.
But, number 20 is in the offing,
Proving, **Verse, is the best of vices__**
Perhaps a good vice, yours to find.

ב

Another Though: If only humankind, would "TURN"
To the experiences found and known,
Then perhaps to all, a better life is shown.

ב

Twists and Turns

Perhaps you think a "Turn or Turns,"
Are not, important premises in life.
Then you would be wrong.
So wrong:
Just ponder, "turn key, turn out, turnover,
Or a turnover (one with icing)."
Drive, the turnpike, go through the turnstile,
See what is on the "turn table."

What's coming at every turn?
Go by turns, in turn, turn back,
Turnabout (fair play and all),
The SOB is a Turn Coat,
Women always use__ a turn down.
Yes "Turn," a mighty four- letter word
(Or "Turns" if used).
And in combination with other words__
Is, a demand for action__
Throughout a lifetime!

"Turn and turns," helps assure, living well
Are paramount;"
Until, that last breath is "turned down!"

 っ

Prayer Time

I pray the words in verse I write,
Able I am in black and white,
To put on paper for a time to come.
And, here for you, reader friend__
Is hope they stimulate your thinking some,
And, if so, then__ my mission is done!
っ

Life's Road

What, time has proven—
That with or without you,
Life travels on.

Changes take place,
New horizons seen,
Wars are fought.

Dying is mean,
Old people disappear,
From the scene—

Babies are born,
And make their stand,
And, they too wither in time.

And the process starts anew.
With, a destination, brought to mind,
And a by-way selected, for the place to find.

So, keep your goal in mind,
For the time you are granted,
And, live well, the life and living to be thine.

Take the time to plan your days,
Work your plan, with good in mind,
Then, chances are, your soul will survive.

Not everything will always, go your way—
But hard work and tenacity,
Can make a difference, at the end of a day.

ב

When, Two, Become One

The lines read: "If mom died tomorrow,
My father couldn't find his socks!"

That in many cases,
Is more truth than fiction__
In each word scribed above.

"How sad! How truly sad__
When the Reaper comes to call,
And leaves chaos in the changing tide."

It could be, a, him, or her,
But in *"Chesapeake Requiem"*
By: Earl Swift,
(By the way, this is, an outstanding book.)
This was a quote,
By one of Tangier Island's women.

Proving, adjustments,
To changes in life,
Is always a challenge supreme.

For when breath is denied one,
The living, are in for__
An extensive learning experience,
Wanted or not.

For many__ make that most,
When married,
And a compartmentalized life exists.
He does his, and she does the rest.

What she knows and does,
He in many cases knows not.
And, vice-versa,

This, the price of bliss__ dutifully paid,
While, many times,
In the back of one's mind__
Questions arise.

Questions few times are discussed,
When they come from daily doing,
And, life goes on__ until it doesn't.

And then one learns
How for two__ one must do__
A new row, is to be plowed.

Just words supplied,
How you treat them,
Is yours to decide.

Hear the adage: "Knowledge is Power."
A true guidepost, to remember.

כ

Clear Thought. For many as we know,
Tomorrow may not come!
But, for most it does__
And a better world is, just a breath, to take.

Tis wise; however, before that last breath comes,
To live a life of goodness,
Or perhaps, if not__ it will be Satan,
The last one you will see.
St. Peter, is the better outcome. Sez, GOD and me!

כ

Growing Times
(Not even close to all)

Pick-up games, on the old back lot,
Left-handers not prized,
Too many balls hit, the skylights,
Of the two-story row homes__
Then rain, found a place to drop.

Up the hill on the left,
Ashton Street,
Paved with cobble stones,
No houses from home plate down.

How many generations__
Had played__ on this oddball__
Piece of ground?
Baseball, football, and sledding__
Down the hill, in wintertime!

There was a time in the mid 1940s,
When the guys from WWII came back.
And were patrons in the Bar,
On Christian Street__
Who, bought us gloves, balls and bats,
Stored there, in a closet overnight.
Two of us at a time,
Were allowed to pass through the Bar,
And, get the equipment out.
Real gloves, and not rocket balls.

Then as 1950 arrived,
The city built a rec-area,
Across the street, from our old ball field
A big plus, for us!
Then, my parents and I moved away,
Funny how those memories remain.

Are almost as vivid today,
As when garnered, in the 1940s.

The move to the Towson area,
I now see as a huge loss,
Of a time in my life,
Never to be gotten again.

Yet, strange how things go,
I kept traveling back,
By bus and street car,
And then with my 1936 Chevrolet.

To spend time,
With, my extended family,
Of West Baltimore.

Then, I married a girl,
I first kept time with (as they say),
When I was just barely 13.
And, she and I had an apartment,
Not too far from our Jr. High School.

I guess it is true,
No matter how far you go,
You can take the boy/girl
Out of Baltimore__

But can't take Baltimore,
Out of them.

My "Bride' now buried,
Just several miles,
From where we once lived,
With, 5 generations of our kin
God, willing someday with her, I will be.

While this may seem a tale of sadness,
It is anything but;
And in books I have written,
I have touched,
On some of the "Growing Stuff."

And, now I think, before it is too late__
So much more, is worth the ink,
To, capture, grand memories__
Of times, never quite like them,
And the guys and gals__
Who made life, so, good, in that space and place.

Of course,
This, is only one mans' prospective.
I hope this bit of writing,
Stirs, great memories, of "your past life."
But color them not__ keep in true black and white.

ↄ

Taking, a "Turn"

Right turn, wrong turn
Conundrums throughout life,
Are, enigmas to solve!
May your "rights"
Always out-number your wrongs__
Or more pain than you would like,
Is what you will make.

Turns you take while living__
Pay the fees, for the gifts received__
For birth, breath and life!

ↄ

Dogs of War

Wouldn't it, be wonderful,
If, never again to see,
The strife, pain and loss, by "War__"
Visited upon Earth evermore.

Note the talent lost in War,
Never to be seen again.
Look at the beauty of lands,
Scared by bombs.

Feel the pain of mothers,
Whose sons' love__
Never again to know!
And, still war, waits to be reborn.

What, is the matter with humankind,
That, learn not from lessons taught__
Time after time, after time__
From battles won and lost.

There is no true winner in "WAR,"
That, a simple truth, known.
Yet, like a bad penny, War,
Is a coin__ ever exposed.

Why not, Muzzle, those **"Dogs of War__"**
Can humankind not see,
If not, they will howl, again.

 っ

A, Thought: It is my belief, Cynics,
are not born__ but shaped__
By those, with an unkind bent.

っ

Boaters' Blues

Ah, the Chesapeake,
A river one time,
Part of the Susquehanna.

Till the last ice age,
And for a while a lake,
Till the Atlantic Ocean had its way.

Today that Bay
For millennia past,
Is, a source of wildlife__
Birds, fish, crustaceans and so much more
And in many ways,
A, "wonder" of beauty__ unmatched.

For many Octobers,
I have marveled at the trees
That surround, in their painted loveliness.
A vision for a "Monet" to paint
And, cameras to find, pure joy, in life.

In "Fall" on a sailboat,
The sun warmed days,
And cool pleasing nights,
Are, a treasure supplied.

Then morning sunrises,
To capture, your heart and mind,
In moments subline.

She the Chesapeake, is a lady of many moods__
And the wise, learn to recognize
Sun, rain, moon, hurricane,
Calms, gales, all in a boater's life
And, be prepared when they are found.

If you are lucky enough,
To be aboard with sails unfurled,
The feeling of freedom, of challenge
Of being a big part of life,
Are, memories caught,
To carry you through,
Many, a long winter night.

And, even if a "Stink Potter"
You happen to be,
C-Bay draws you in!
If it is autumn__ then open those
Engines up wide, for perhaps,
The last time before, snow flies.
And likely you will be forgiven,
For the short time__
Your surrounds, you pollute.

This, just a ragman's joke__
To help reduce pain,
Of putting the boat up,
As most say good bye
To another boating year.

The stark black and white,
Of winter on the Bay,
Is beauty in its own right!
Fewer see this delight.

Oh Lord, hear this prayer I make,
About, Global Warming, & Climate Change;
Give us all the will__
The Chesapeake Bay to save,
For the unborn generations, yet unmade!

ᄃ

"Turn," Back Time

More than once in a while,
My mind "turns" back__
To the years between 1974 through 1991.

And, memories flood to the surface__
And the star of those vignettes
Is, a ragamuffin mutt of a dog;
Chosen by my wife__ as a gift,
For our almost; eight- year-old son.

Half toy poodle, and half toy collie/beagle__
Runt of the litter, but big on personality.
Truly the best damn dog ever__
Stories about him, to us are legendary.

In this month now of October,
Thirty plus years after his passing,
The memory of "Rusty" is alive and well.
In that son, who will be 56 this year,
As will our onetime, next- door neighbor__
And those guys are still friends!

And Just a year or so ago,
Both or their families including me,
Got together, for dinner,
And the tales, of a wagging tail,
Began, before the last bite was done.

Melancholy I am at this moment,
For I can't believe the boys, are in their mid 50s
With families' near grown!
And, me, tear in eye, for dog, nay forgotten,
One, truly, a treasured family member.

つ

Talent in Turn

Everyone, a talent, does have.
Many, times it, is hidden away,
And, the first challenge is__
To, ascertain; "what it is."

Sometimes it is apparent,
And, other times, truly a conundrum.
Mine was hidden for years,
And, then one day,
When in loss, it surprised me to be.

And what a gift,
At least to me__ to find,
In a time, most appropriate.
Got yours, then that is grand,
No__ then search till found,
And could be,
A better life, you, it will astound.

Talent in every size and shape
First, you must know it__ to appreciate__
And even if the world doesn't agree,
That should not matter to thee__
It's your talent, not theirs!

But, if others see in you,
And praise comes your way__
You have won a prize__
To brighten the rest, of your days.
Mine? Is, writing short stories in verse,
And even then, thought "one, & done"
That was a half dozen years ago.
My books, number 20, with covers on!

ᑣ

Green Wood Telegraph

In years long ago,
Smoke was rising in the still air,
Puff long, puff, puff, short,
Puff, puff, puffs, for, it was, a long report.

Miles away a receiver read,
And then puffed, it on,
It said, that Native Americans,
Were to fight,
To save their land and way of life.

We all know how that turned out.
Now, tis water over the dam__
Mostly because, Native Americans,
Had no, immigration Policy.

Sort of like today, here in the USA__
Illegals, and liberals,
Who, pander, common sense.

And the law__ refuses to read,
"The writing on the wall."

Y'all come,
For we don't care,
If you tear the country down!
Here take the dollars,
Others earned,
And, burn up the Constitution,
That worked fine
For two hundred plus years.

For in a short time,
Could we, a 3rd world country__ be?

As the last of those,
Who, have held the line,
Will be buried and gone,
And then, see what you find.

Back to the "Dark Ages"
And maybe someday,
Perhaps, humankind, just might,
Bring forth, men like Washington,
And Jefferson, and others of their ilk__
To give freedom, another, try.

And, smarter maybe__ be,
To enforce, the tenet of democracy__
(while we still be a Republic.)
And, credit goes to those__
Who brought the good about.

And there are no rights,
Unless earned or re-earned,
Each and every day and night.

History is no mystery__
Its facts carefully kept and reviewed.
If it is the will, not to let the sociopaths__
Lead anyone, down the "garden" path.

To that end, maybe "War" has a place
But, always there__ is a better way,
Than War, and the loss of life & limb.

A great dream, and a prayer, to abide.
When the Washington crowd__
Sees, themselves not__ as "Royalty"
<u>**Could be then, we be again a true USA.**</u>

ᆨ

Statements

Life, if granted to you__
Then living, is what you must do;
How, that you do__
Is a story__ each day to unfold.

But to live not for just that day__
But to think, look and prepare,
For the challenges to face,
All along__ life's way.

Each day you arise,
Give thought, to treasure;
Every moment, breath is allowed.
Live, love, be kind, be thankful,
For all gifts arrayed.

Learn something or much__
New and useful each day alive__
And so much more,
To show, you care, about being alive.

Everything written here,
You should already know,
And even much more__
So, write the "more" down.

And read, and reread,
And, make it a habit this to do.
Then, what a grand citizen__
You, will be!

And, this say I, as a prayer to go with thee.

ב

One-Minute, Review

In the next minute__
Someone will fall in love.
Some others, will wave goodbye.
Some be born and others die.
Many will see the world,
With a jaundiced eye.

Most, will live an ordinary life__
Doing some good,
And, perhaps a little bad,
Others will the "game" play__
In politics, with a known name__
This and more__ we call life.

The list goes on__
For the surface, is just barely scratched!
Think of the history written,
By those alive today,
Which will be added__
To all history, known from mans' first day.

How much history is repeated,
Because attention to detail__
Was lost in the fray?
Will humankind ever wise up,
Before Earth has its last day?
You; are needed, to help lead the way.

Tomorrow will come, if the universe stays,
Tomorrow will be better, if effort is made,
Today, and every day, is first to be played.

ɔ

An Old Man's Ramblings
(Conversation with an older friend, now gone!)

I think now,
That age has come upon me,
And am no longer,
Physically, what I used to be.
I, in wonder, if ever,
Those "youthful adventures,"
I once had,
I somehow could do again?

Just a foolish paging of thoughts,
As a memory or two,
Returns from the recess' of my mind!
Fun they were in their time,
Fulfilling youth's needs__
And, they were once__ mine.

Those__ I would like to do again__
Not new things, of the daring do__
That many do today.
But a repeat of those, once done,
And the way, they, made me feel__
In those, wonderful bye gone days.

Of course, I know,
With the aches and pains
I now face each day,
Doing again are wishes,
Not to be done, by me.

But I like many
Think a dream and a memory__
Worth the time to hope, could be;
Ah, an old Man's revery.

What, makes life grand
Is the belief in miracles.
Yes, I know these thoughts border on__
Well, you know, what, I mean.
But, if there is a message,
Within these lines__ do take it to heart.

Don't delay, "get out and do,"
Whatever you can,
Whether it be little, or much
Time once gone,
Isn't ever, found again.

So, remember,
You can't live life over,
Unless you have memories,
Already made.

So, make a new memory, everyday__
Amazing then, the comfort,
In reliving them again and again!

Thanks for taking the time,
To hear my diverse thoughts,
I hope you get the gist of them!
I only shared them,
So, you can understand,
What in time might be yours, to view!

So, let not a minute, get away from you.
They are yours
But, don't take them for granted,
While they seem many,
You, too soon will understand__
They are truly too damn few!

ↄ

A, Turn of Truth

No true musician, will I ever be__
But, to read musical notes,
A, true joy, would be!
Then, I could follow,
The parade of music played.

Unfortunately, I have little musical talent
For an, instrument to play__
Or, read the notes jotted down.
And, in this life, I understand__
For me, it will always be, this way.

Oh, but in this living every day,
I am surrounded with talent__
And, enjoy all I can find.
For, at least the beat is mine,
And the music is held in my mind.

Second best, but so grateful am I
That, others can and do__
Sing, and play__
And, I feel, they do it for me.
This I sense, is for me__ what can be.

ל

Heed

Step out, step up, and step forward,
Challenges make life worthwhile__
Tis, time__ to be alive.
Should you sit and do nothing__
Then note: **"eternity" is a long boring ride.**
Find and live, tis the reason, you are alive.

ל

Do a Good Turn

How many times, do you
Turn__ each day?
No idea' you say.

But "turns," in your life__
Are a challenge arrayed,
And, a big role in your living,
Each and every day.

Have you ever really given
"Turns" the merest of thoughts__
As you travel along life's way?

For your own sake, I pray__
Do give *"turn and turns"*
A place in you daily thoughts,
Then put those thoughts to work.

For, it's your *"turn!"*
To make the right *turn*,
Each time a *turn* must be made.

ב

Free Advice

Success requires large doses,
Of, inspiration and perspiration__
Spare neither,
To assure, ensure and insure
A good life__ to secure.

ב

A Question Asked

Will, we ever be able__
To "will" a talent,
Saved from one, to an heir?

Or is that a dream__
To remain unfulfilled?

If not, why not,
When so many strides,
In every direction today,
Are, seen and done.

The answer: perhaps, known, is "**NO.**"
For talent when the one is done,
Is lost in mind and DNA,
When the holder's,
Last breath is taken away.

But will we not someday,
Be able to be capture,
Strands of another's DNA__
And pass it along on life's way?

What a gift to the world,
That would surely be!
My thoughts with Music and Art, start__
But there would be no limit,
If that possibility could be.

Just think of:
A Mozart in centuries to come,
Or a Monet, more brush strokes to find,
The list is endless,
And, and begs no end, once begun.

But, to assure the value,
Of the future to come___
One caveat, would be subscribed:
Only one heir at a given time___
But would that not, keep hope alive?

Just a thought, a dream,
But unfortunately, somehow,
An evil doer, would find a way___
To bring back, some of the Devil's spawn
And screw up, this possible good idea?

Then again; just perhaps, a boon to man!

ꜫ

Words Overheard or Said

"Hey, it's good to see you!
Words bandied about,
For unnumbered times
By people throughout the Universe.

One would imagine, it was so
More than not___ but is it?

Or is it just words to say,
A seemingly, hearty statement,
While inside, you wishing they would go away.

Ah, forget it,
Just playing "Devil's Advocate"
On dark and stormy day!

Or, am I?

ꜫ

Write Now

I admire those, who the time, do take,
With, fortitude_ almost daily,
A log or a diary_ keep.

Willing to capture the moments
Their thoughts, there inscribed,
Recognizing, they perhaps each word_ worth,
Review, in some future time.

Memories are good and grand; however,
So, many are lost in a foggy-mind.
But when a word or two is captured
In ink, on paper, then can be reread;
Maybe be a gem, recovered_ down the line.

A, word or three, can and will_
Jump-start the mind and memories;
Of places, times and people once known,
Crisp and clear, as if taking place now,
Even if happened in decades, long ago.

Yes, keeping a log,
Is, many times an onus_
And too easily, put aside.

But the payoff when one does_
Is, the words of that moment.
Could be worth their weight in gold.
And the effort and time in ink to inscribe.

In my days now of writing,
When just a glimmer of memory,
Makes a call, how I wish, time I had taken_
To capture life's tidbits, in ink_
When, I thought I knew it all.

Maybe one good reader,
Will take my thoughts and run!
Not now, but sometime in the future__
Seeing the truth, of my words__ here spun.

The ink on paper in your days to come,
Will, pay dividends to you;
But today, you know not, Who__
Is that "WHO" you will become?
So, it behooves you__
to make "you" a "Good" one.

ᛑ

Tick Tock

Clocks of all type,
If fit to run,
Keep the time as Earth is spun,
Numerically, tell when day is done,
And, even when night,
Turns away from, daylight sun!

Aren't clocks a wonderful thing?
But I can't help but wonder,
If time is a perpetual thing
That without a clock,
And its alarm to ring__
Would, time stop,
In places known.
And there'd be,
No more__
Living
Things?

ᛑ

Time to Turn

Why, is it that "man"
Cannot truly spell Peace?
Just five letters,
Three vowels and two consonants
And yet, Humankind__
Time and time again__
Will, bring disgrace to that word__

Not so much the word__
But, the living thereof, the ideal;

And, to those who,
Wish it be, long lasting__
Find, it only in times deemed short__
Before fools, tarnish the peacemaker's art.

"PEACE" a word, of meaning and majesty,
Poetry on the tongue, freedom to live,
And, Somehow, someday to grasp by all.

Tis almost impossible,
For, humankind, to keep it, in place__
for, any length of time,
To be fully appreciated,
By generations, yet to come.

Perhaps, true peace for all__ never;
Because of an apple, and a serpent,
As told, in the Christian Bible.

How much be true,
And, how much be bias of man,
Who inked, the scrolls
In those, ancient times!

How stupid are the world's humans__
Not to take a stand, and see the wisdom,
Imbued in his/her conscience.

And the potential, of true__ brotherhood,
With, equality of races and sexes of all humankind.
Only, to allow Satan (if that be your belief)
To deny it, for generations yet to be seen.

A Life that could be__ by taking the "right" turn!

ב

Turn On

Now, to be honest with you__
For an honest man I hope I am
For that was what I was raised to be.

I tell you words,
That 'would be wise,
For you to hear and heed,
And then perhaps,
Honest like "Abe" you would see me, to be.

Here they are, as simple can be:
Never, never a politician be,
For your tongue, will grow,
As long, as the nose
On, Pinocchio!

And, no sane person,
Will, your words then believe.
Period; the best in truth,
Comes to you, from me!

ב

Science doesn't, Lie

I looked upon a mountain,
In a foreign land__
Photographed in a newscast,
Showing a melting glacier.

The mountain now nothing but rock,
With buildings attached,
That, visitors would stay,
When looking at__
The glacier that__ had been there,
For centuries, history did say.

There was a sense of panic,
In those who the story told,
That after losing the ice support,
The bare rocks of the mountain,
Would soon crack and fold.

I know not, if this thought holds true,
But the French people,
In whose land the glacier had been__
Were worried, and, could see,
What, Global Warming & Climate Change__
Could actually do!

Without question, tis, past the time,
To "turn away", from the truth.
And, if not, too late, for all in the world,
To face, temperature rise is a human fault__
And, that before our fate would be sealed,
On this orb of "Eden" we call Earth__
Action is the reaction, needed by one & all.
Before our non-action, becomes a true curse.

ʖ

"Understand"

There is a core of fear
Deep in everyone!
Hide if you truly can,
But it is there to contend.

Coming from the moment
When humankind the swamp__
Did leave, those millions of years ago__
For, life on land__ was new to know.

That fear, deep rooted,
In common sense,
Of the moment,
A new world was begun.

And, what was to be faced,
With each step to make,
As the human species,
Adapted and changed__
With little idea,
What tomorrow, would make.

And, here we stand today,
With nagging fears,
That, forward still arrive__
And most, are caused by humankind,
Who defies__ Nature's workable plan.

And let avarice,
And common sense, be "over-come".
Thus, he/she, refuses to see, that "brotherhood"
Is the answer for true peace,
if and when done.

ᔕ

Possible or Not

Not everything is up,
Nor is everything down,
(Down only seems that way).
Most of the time both average out.
But it is the "ups," for a better life,
Even downs, show you this is the way.

I hope this gets through to you__
Why you ask?
You don't know me,
But I am a fan of "yours."
And, we share the same air__ we breathe.

I don't care your tint of skin,
Your race, sex or creed,
Only that you try__
To live the brotherhood dream.
For in the long term, and a good life,
All must truly believe!

For millions of years
Humankind hasn't been able,
To breathe life into Brotherhood,
And that, is the "**crime of humanity.**"
Perpetrated__ on unborn generations.

Our insides are interchangeable__
And, yet we allow, pigment of skin,
And, nuisances of life,
And, other minor things__
Separate the potential of all humankind.

Tis no wonder "War" is a daily thing__
When stupidity is prevalent in humankind.

When with the brains
And conscience, so granted,
We still make not__
A better world, for all of life thereon.
Where "all" could exist and thrive,

What truly cogent reason,
Can we claim, for, not today living__
In, total peace and harmony?

Oh, if only we would, wash away'__
The Biases of Humankind.

↺

"So"

In this day and time,
Most, everyone can **read** & **"write"**
But, like everything in life,
Some do whatever, better than others!

However, one will never know,
What, can be done__
Unless and until many "things,"
Are, tried__ many times,
And failed until found sound.

So, one perhaps should,
"Take a TURN"
At whatever comes to mind,
That can **turn** one on!
Who knows, what will__ **Turn** "up,"
Before daylight subsides!

↺

The Circle of Life

To emphasize, the importance__
Of the thought to be conveyed,
Is hopefully, a help, for you to gain.

First, death is just a part of living__
And, paying prior to need,
Makes living life, before demise,
And easier "road" to run!

When my father passed,
Those many years before__
The "dollars" at the time, not easy to score.
We as a family, then determined, a better way.

This, became an extended family funeral plan,
That served us well, as years have passed.
Knowing, coverage required, was there,
At the time, when sadness blurred the mind.

So, when my mother passed,
It was just three days before,
Our youngest son was to marry.
Mom, in Maryland,
Our son in Massachusetts,
And, my wife and I, in Buffalo, New York.

This had all the makings for a disaster,
And, was a concern, important to us__
Not to disrupt the status Quo.
It was clear, in those days before__
We truly had done, the wise and right thing__
Then, with one phone call, and looking ahead.
The arranged, detailed and pre-paid__
Funeral expenses, had the situation under control.
And this again, in 2008, for my Mother-in-Law.

Perhaps this, is an idea for you__
To save pain, at a time of deep sadness.
And by paying ahead,
Cost at the time, is guaranteed.

You, select what you want, you pay up front,
Or borrow, elsewhere, so the "trust,
Is earning dividends immediately, and the deed is done.

You are going to pay someday. <u>*Do it, now!*</u>
Pay less, by a lot. Then, worry, less through life.

And depending on the time invested,
There is, Usually, dollars left for other expenses.
Review, check the small print, and prepay.
Wise words, for even wiser actions.
It's a common sense and wise investment.

ב

All Depends on Choice

Just a "turn" to the right from wrong,
Might be the choice in life to make!
Chances are, good, by measuring__
The potential success of a "turn"
Then, your life will turn out__ Right.

And, if you must another turn to take,
Because the last one, was a dead-end__
Knowledge gained from past turns,
Will most likely, "turn out" better then.
For turns, are teachers in their time__
A gift to you. from an ever, patient God!

ב

Always, a Surprise

She was standing at the shoreline,
Staring at the sunset,
Completely enraptured,
Her surroundings, captured in silence.

I could not take my eyes from her,
Her light brown shimmering hair.
Breathing slowly,
Not willing to disturb the moment,
The sun, about the horizon to drop.

Then, her faun made a sound,
And this beautiful doe,
Woke to reality,
And the two__ mother and fawn,
Turned toward the woodland.

Catching sight of me, stared;
And with grace, seemed to nod,
"Turned" and walked away!

No hurry in her step,
It seemed to me,
A mutual feeling of peace__
We had shared.
You never know,
When a special moment,
Will come your way.

Somewhat, like, the photo,
Of, my wife and my son__
On my den wall displayed.
When, I turn on the den light.

She and he__ are there, to greet me,
Just a shadowed photo of two playing chess__
From those many years gone away.
I wish all__ could have,
A captured moment__
One of those special days!

ב

Seeing Memories

I look around our home__
To me, still ours,
She, gone now for many years.

And I see, her artful Afghans,
Curtains, needlepoint,
And photos here and there__
And, so much more,
And think, I had, been truly blessed__
With her my "Bride" for many years.

I try to keep her flowers and plants,
Inside and out alive__
And, the house, as if she was to return.

A friend recently said to me:
I am surprised you never re-married.
My immediate reply__
When you have had the best,
Who needs to test the rest.
But having friends,
Is a different thought to provide.

ב

Time for a Turn-around

I wish I could say,
That, my favorite season,
Was, living up
To its reputation, gained.

For several seasons past,
Those colors extraordinary
Which, autumn paints—
Across our land,
Just haven't been "found."

Now I don't blame this on
Autumn's landscape painting team,
For I know full well,
It is Mother Nature,
Who has put a pox, on the land.

Showing her anger, against man,
She, then in summer's doldrums,
Rained deluges from the sky
And then followed, with heat oppressive,
To cook, and drown all the green found.

But two years, is two times, too much,
I want, my fall season's—
Reds, yellows, gold and crimsons—
In array on trees around,
And the green contrast, of the evergreens.

I need, the beauty of fall,
To, brighten my day—
Before winter's cold and snow descends.
I need the pure aroma of the season,
And not, the odor, of brown leaves down.

Oh, for the painted beauty,
Against the azure blue sky,
Yes, autumn in its glory,
Is prayer, I send to God.

Oh, Lord, give humankind the wisdom,
To stop the devastation,
We have unleashed, upon Mother Earth,
And, return from Global Warming,
And Climate Change, to an equilibrium__
Known, not that long ago, on this orb called Earth.

Here me oh citizens, one and all;
This and much more, is for "us" to undo,
Since, we, humankind, are the culprit in view.

ס

Rhetorical

No "one" is an island__
We are all   of Terri Fermi somewhere found.
For we are not fish, nor mammals of the sea,
But an image of the one__ believed.
And, what you believe, Is sacrosanct for thee.

But, look around and see this world__
In all its majesty, and remember,
Someone or something, gave you, life,
And you, should have the wisdom__ that, to see.
The question then is:
What, are we, here to do__
And Why not is the doing, being done?

ס

A New Leaf, to Turn

If you, had your life to live over,
Would you change__
The life you have known?
A good question to propose.

If you say yes,
Then this just might be the time,
For you, to get__
Your head, screwed on right__
And, to be, the person,
You truly this day__
Could, should__ would be known.

What a great opportunity, to have__
That changes are a must to be made,
With, the possibility, at hand,
That you could play a roll,
In making a better world.

No__ would be lie,
For you already know,
There is room for you,
To be better, than you are.
However, It does take effort__
Can and will you__ the effort, provide?

The Devil, is watching
And licking his chops,
For he is betting__ you will not.

Only you, can prove, him wrong__
And, do what you know now__ is right!

ט

www.ingramcontent.com/pod-product-compliance
Lightning Source LLC
Chambersburg PA
CBHW060204050426
42446CB00013B/2988